A Way Less Travelled

Also by Adrian Rogers and published by Ginninderra Press
The Sun Behind the Sun
Between Two Hemispheres
The Prisoner's Messenger
The Medicine Wheel
Music is a River of Life
Seasons, Situations and Symbols (Pocket Poets)
Human Nature & the Welfare State (Pocket Polemics)
Croagh Patrick (Pocket Places)
Port Victoria (Pocket Places)

Adrian Rogers

A Way Less Travelled

A Way Less Travelled
ISBN 978 1 76041 884 7
Copyright © text Adrian Rogers 2020
Cover photo: Greg Larcombe from Pixabay

First published 2020 by
GINNINDERRA PRESS
PO Box 3461 Port Adelaide 5015 Australia
www.ginninderrapress.com.au

Contents

Part 1: The Way is Hard, But Blake Understands

When the Flood Comes – in a Dream	9
Croagh Patrick Pilgrimage	10
Blake's 1st Vision – The Wailing Wall	11
Overgrown Track	12
Blake's 2nd Vision – Beneath the Foundations	13
On Higher Ground	14
Blake's 3rd Vision – Mount Moriah	15
The Night Train to Nowhere	16
Blake's 4th Vision – The Holy Sepulchre	17
At the Crossroads	18
Blake's 5th Vision – The Dome of the Rock	19
By the Water – Mirror in Mirror	20
Blake's 6th Vision – The Temple of Humanity	21

Part 2: Goodbye Blake, More Toil Ahead

On a Desert Track	25
Elemental Evocations – Earth	26
Passing Over	27
The Cave – a Mithraic Refuge	28
After Passing – Blake Brings Light and Peace	29
Yellow Rose	30
Promenade – the Eternal Migrant	31
Down the Roadways of the Years	32
Oasis	33
By the River and the Ford	34
The Wave Rider's Revelation	35
Candle in the Dark	36
Siren Sea Song	37
Self-examination on a Winding Path	38

Part 3: After the Last Post

Last Post – Anzac Day	43
By-path	44
Nightfall Memories	45
Cold Night Bells	46
Into the Dawn	47
Cantilena Pacifica	48
Beyond the Margin	49
The Loneliness of the Long Distance Runner	50

Part 4: There is a River

Autumn Processional	53
The Traveller Meets Gregory the Great	55
Recessional Winter	56
John Tavener Confronts the Traveller	58
Spring Rounds	59
Die Winterreise & Die Lindenbaum	61
Saraband of Summer	62
There is a River	64

Part 1

The Way is Hard, But Blake Understands

When the Flood Comes – in a Dream

Sodden-leaved autumn, root slippery
half strips branches rain seeping,
no misted magically veiling
mellow fruitfulness
only a thinly winding path down-sloped,
levelling, breaking into a clearing
as water rising
laps over fear's primal rashness
devoid of rational lightening,
dreaming a path's aloneness
neither hearth nor home remembered
until disquiet
is dismembered by hope
grounded, upraised, sky cleared,
rending
lead-like weighted clouds slung low
yellow sun-shafted,
defining the alchemy of confidence
rectifying a mind's scope
as lead to gold, mastering
the unexpected
yet present tensed, dry grounded
as trees draw back;

a higher clearing…

Croagh Patrick Pilgrimage

…until tossed clouds incense-like
over-roll a rough stone track,
a mountain hare wraith-silent appears
disappears
amid small stone rattles

a cold-edged self as the soul battles
fears, a clouded unknowing
with bloodied stones
no inspiration but pain,
desire's silent pressuring,
bones slipping across hard surfaces

and life/death interfaces
with thunder, lightning, rain,
attacking those sheltering places
fourteen stations of the Cross

while exorcising our loss
unto nowhere
by a sunburst above the Temple
when the clouds power down

everywhere.

Blake's 1st Vision – The Wailing Wall

Peace, be the dove
hovering above a wall
of stone-embedded prayers
remnant
of a universal temple unfinished

and undiminished
touch heads, hearts, and hands
in hope, the constant flame
returning to its source
simple as truth, absolute.

Make us resolute
in fellowship.
May those who stay to feed the soul
and those who seek
for green lands far away
go their ways in peace.

Shalom
my brother, my sister, my love.

Overgrown Track

An overgrown track through minds awake
commands not
a spread-running growth of creepers
green/brown wet clinging
moss coating on rough barked trunks,
millennium lengths of dead leaf littering
the undergrowth
and overgrowth
of lichens drooping, grey/ghostly appearing
through half veiled cloud trails
falling to treetop level.

A way lightens and darkens through shake
and watery rot
of underfoot deadness, but sleepers
commune with changes ringing
as the shaken one dunks
with wetness those glittering
eyes-wide memories, the sloth
of neither and both.
Hearts welcoming pain without fearing
grasp at the rigging of love's gilded sails,
sun and moon mesh to bevel
the gears of conscience,
light glitters on trees, and in lees
at the bottom of a barrel.

Blake's 2nd Vision – Beneath the Foundations

Below Jerusalem
working tools echoing
spark/striking stone in Jerusalem above
clearing the site
stirring the dust of centuries
fall slowly into a crack revealing a vault

and our knowing in trust calls a halt
for fears of fools revealing
what wisdom was concealing.

We hone our skills
assuming not time's unhinging
the thrills of discovery
shifting stones, admitting light,
self-lowering into dark depths,
seeking, finding…

neither treasure nor rust, just
'that', in the vault of the soul.

On Higher Ground

A sun-smitten green-lengthened ridge
gashing the skyline
white-yellows light-mellows slopes
ripped open by grey weathered
brokenly tooth-like rocks
above dark forest waves falling back
like breakers unable to breach the high tops
and the wind
singing over a bridge
onto dreaming, a fine line
crossed when a silent wolf lopes
from the wood, and untethered
sheep, panicked by terrorising shocks
see the hireling flee
and a rack outstretched comes apart
fear stops the flowering of hope
that knowledge might be
and courage find its reward,
until stolen and unloosed
from cleft-scored rocks
is…unknown, yet alone the real.

Blake's 3rd Vision – Mount Moriah

In heaven/earth's interspace
the gold of transformation is
above the world's foundation stone
a lonely road of sacrifice,
conscience an uncertain goad
through dust, sandstorm, fear,

Taurus into Aries passing near
no ram for offering in Aquarius
merely another hilltop destination;
a climb, an altar, a war?

'Lay not thine hand upon the lad…'

while creation holds in store
swarming constellations –
half their story untold,
sewn beneath which
a multitude of generations
all birthrights sold were sacrificed
the seed of ages
voiceless on history's pages.

The Night Train to Nowhere

Iron on iron hypnotises
sleepers on the night train to nowhere
sleeping minds synthesises
serpentine, long in scope everywhere
beyond hope messaging all comers
from the outermost edges of winters
and summers, layered universes,
mind driving wedges between sleeping
and waking, consciences shaking
like windblown sedges and garden hedges

iron rails emerging
through darkness surging
echoing postmodern mechanising
for dreamers digitising
casting confetti
poets devising opera libretti,
weddings, births, deaths,
famous last words, last breaths,
scheming imaginers texting, fingering
for financial advantages lingering
hypochondriacs fearing infection
spirits perhaps seeing
the Bridge to Resurrection,
all drop their cover
or sleep till the earth turns over.

Blake's 4th Vision – The Holy Sepulchre

A beating sun echoes
voices from the stones
shielding an interior's
low light down-dimmed
shafted lamps slimmed
delicate pulsations
in-drawing yet emanating
a heart responding glow

softening a show
of silence ambient in tone
amplifying the day
hallowing the night

sanctifying a soul light
at the point of intersection
where fire is new
and a stone rolled back
for resurrection.

At the Crossroads

A cloud-cold-loomed greyness
over shadowy crossways is soul-desert bleak
and watchers
by heartfelt indecision prompted
considering the imponderable
twinned dark, light,
not always holy ones but over-lookers
behind the dark yet mitigating lightness
are palpably invisible
to those seeking only materiality
the concision of the verifiable,
searching by the checkerboard, sons
and onlookers.

Above the crossroads sobriety is a low sky
and Mercury, rewarded with votive offerings
chorused by wild, wind-borne voices
serenading oncoming night
asks, 'Along which road will dicing fortunes try
these travellers, desert, forest, sufferings,
pleasures? Do roads offer choices,
hopes bright?'

Apparitions will not answer from without
only within, along perception's fine line thin
stretching into light.

Blake's 5th Vision – The Dome of the Rock

Gold circled perfection in the light is an ascending paradox.
Can a place of sacrifice be a stepping stone to resurrection?

Enlightened perfection is release, a stumbling block, a contradiction.
Is Jerusalem world centred, or a rock of offence?

An octagon extrapolates the law of One, and reaction intense
the Three, but on whose summit will freedom's banner be unfurled?

From its eminence, shall memory and majesty be hurled
or the Dome, the Sepulchre, the Wailing Wall be at peace?

When the Mount is lightning struck, the Dead Sea's release
is a healing, all futures are signed, sealed,
and in an eye-blink the Golden Gate opened;
whose entering shall be the ultimate returning?

By the Water – Mirror in Mirror

Water mirroring
condensing fluidity
eternally restless limpidity
glitter-sparking, translucent
earth, sky, star bursting,
emerging

images sun/moon crossing over
depths greened, golden,
blue pastel, unclouded,
cloudy, reflectively
resonantly percussively
a north/south musicality
blending tonalities
in-tuning to mysteries
east, west,
luminously mirroring
the self all-knowing
in flight soaring
centred.

Blake's 6th Vision – The Temple of Humanity

I am raised by hearts and hands
but not in stone.

Worn to the bone
my builders toil in sweat and blood
yet I am
Eternal in the Heavens.

The yeast of endeavour leavens
the bread of humanity.

Serenity and sanity
envision a temple not made with hands.

I have bands
to bind the heart,
I, Jerusalem above.

Approach me in love
along the star path, brother, sister,
be builders in peace
under the sign of the dove.

Part 2

Goodbye Blake, More Toil Ahead

On a Desert Track

A taunting sun strikes out at shaded eyes
glaring
as though flaring off polished brass
white blazing
unmercifully hazing earth, stone,
and wind wisps breath-stirring the track's dust…

at a temple in ruins?

A foot stumbling on a boulder
attention draws from relentless scrutinisers,
heat/light berating
head/shoulder coverings, skin, a gaze sharp,
intense, thin,
yet colder than memorial moments
seeing the stone inscribed
too hot to touch under an unmercifully
meridian flaunting sun unable to arrest
a fierce glance
at chiselled runes outstandingly out-staring
upwardly,
yet against this meridian passing
the Temple rises, no freak of history
when light slants, the ruins speak…

Elemental Evocations – Earth

…as red roses blooming
into stillness and light pulsing
rhapsodise earth messages
evoking songs of summer
her shapers seldom seen
crafting elementally
their chiming, rhyming,
thyme scenting diffusing spells
through dancing hours

cast earth offerings
before remembered ones
imagined as garden gnomes
yet animate, and more
in passing like rays of light
before the Gates
of Capricorn or Cancer
onwards to Lammas harvesting.

Catch a falling star
call out and watch red, green,
blue, white, splendours
light-born dew caught
silvered in the star's wake
trailing, interplay
on rising levels of reality.

Passing Over

I, the Angel of Death
pass over the blood of millennia
for the sake of exiles returning
before the judgments of fire,
cold, and pole shift
decimate
the liars, deniers, traders in justice.

Against injustice my breath
is a feather on the wind of desire
Synagogue of Satan
shaking your shifting foundations.

Victims remember the falling shot
between tower walls,
the Mount of Olives splitting in two
the Destroying Angel
the decimating sacrifice

but for once exiled generations
the Tree of Life.

The Cave – a Mithraic Refuge

Beneath a scourging desert light's hard scrutiny
a grit-grounded track unwinds.

Up-sweeping sloped rock walls and the intensity
of illusion's sidelong dance as the heat unbinds

perceptions of substance, mirage-phasing
a day by day long day by day long…

pilgrim's grinding struggle against a dazing
heat and light's denial of softness, a strong

refusal of sentence remission; inquisitions going
and coming, faces rock hard yet dissolving

the matter of pilgrimage, reaping and sowing,
reckoning and resolving.

A north slope cave mouth is a hill's dark stain,
potentially a resting place for limitlessness

in contemplation, temporal relief from the pain
of inward burning, freed consciousness

rebirth illumined into mindfulness.

After Passing – Blake Brings Light and Peace

Jerusalem of many vistas
choose not the warrior's way,
the Pleiades – for light and peace
sweet influences

mark how the confluences
of holy and material things release
from a miscarriage of regret
the aching hearts of exiles
returning, treading with lightness
their stone studded, praying miles

heeding not the logical wiles
of reason, when petitions
at the Wailing Wall
stall not in offering; calling
as the prophets say for futures
consecrated to war's decease.

Brother, sister, be at peace,
let the marriage feast begin.

Yellow Rose

Beyond the wire that once was
'The Yellow Rose of Texas'
in imagination romps across
spring pale primroses
contending with sun-flamed
winter wattle memories

like light cooled,
solidified, fragmented
into fragile substance
over wet/dry surfaces
generous as scattered largesse

in three seasons fooled
into countenancing
triumph and tragedy's
ephemeral splendours
seasonably rose-like,
dying yet renewable…

Promenade – the Eternal Migrant

…but love is enough,
or is it?

Is love the eternal migrant
between places,
changes, faces,
time bound in consciousness?

Can it tread down
The Last Enemy,
rise like ivy
from lovers tombs
entwined…forever?

Down the Roadways of the Years

A sun boisterous
stages the dance of the hours
fire/flash flickering off polished brass
leading the local band through towns
memorial aspirations
processions longways winding
or straight stretching miles
for marching ghosts, their powers gone
beyond the bickering chatter of the now.

'They shall not pass'...
speech banned, dismissed,
with victory to those living strong
yet their place well earned
is long out-strung
down the roadways of the years
'Days of our lives' and theirs
no fears touching them
just Death with grace
taking a bow
resonantly soft-striking a silencing bell

and for each ghostly shell
of a once living material self, Lord,
Grant them eternal rest
The Last Post, lights out, let it be.

Oasis

Heat shapes forming along a desert track
are shimmer-dancing
mirage enhancing,
a bacchanalian corps de ballet's
riotously silent non-event
eliminating horizon outlines
never lacking shape-shifting glance-back
wraith-like motions, prancing,
taunting, unreasoning
yet seeing a wished-for greenness, away
beyond the mind's consent
a going and coming defining
configured hope

the unveiled scope
of imagination's proven realities
shrinking distances
in the Oasis, where a trope
of water-flows, birdcalls, summoning
and endeavour sharpened
by defining all, instances eternity
conceived
under the palms, where my form
is shadow grey, the lake soul deep,
the self one, its harvest ready to reap…

By the River and the Ford

…until the gorge sides, their steepness
a smothered abruptness
of forty shades greening
jostling-for-space-tree-clustered
crowd a blue/grey
fast flashing river flow's
haphazard tumbling over stones

a track winds deferentially
between water and wood.

The air's cave-echo-like thunderous
stone-on-water voice
afternoon lit, a wild keening
impressionistic chorus mustered,
overawing
where waters clash
in shows of force dividing
on the bones of memory
catches unheedingly
on sky-edging sight
where none have stood.

A rough narrow rock-sliding ford
checks hope's shallow treachery…

The Wave Rider's Revelation

…until scorching-to-glass desert heat
glare-reflective rocks and sands
oven hot are worlds away
banished
by panoramic skyscapes overruling
a limitlessly cooling white-winged sea

where, like Alcuin in hope I might be
on a windswept firm sanded openness
awaiting the onset of a silent dawn

where every wave, a promise shorn
of illusion creates a song,
a hill, a valley, a reason to rally
ghosts from the past in black
and white; light-masking mists
slow-fast magicians daylong nightlong
impersonally non-judgemental, until
from deceit and delusion reborn
by the feeling shocks
of revelation, contemplating,
over stones breaking

'All' is 'One', the soul remaking
and I am…

Candle in the Dark

…where small lights for meditating
in darkness uplit or shaded,
pierced by almost liquid flames
alive infinitely in speaking silence,
of things hoped for the substance
recollected
in burn-rising incense

and cold stone plays attacking games
against silent concentration
aimed at away-tricking stray thoughts
from submissions
to admissions tame

in light wavering, lame,
into thoughts flowing, inwardly intoning
inaudibly denying inhibitions

and moonlight window-thin is shafted
as stars place-change in the shivering dark,
cold beats up, hands shield a spark

I have made my mark…

Siren Sea Song

…so foot tapped hardness is temporary relief
from amorphously inclusive
forest-rooted wetness,
leaf, earth and stones until the break-free,
slipping out

onto a wildly flowing mind-escaping
seascape outreaching
pummelling a flatly resistant
pebble-dashed sandscape.

Freedom from immutability, rule, belief
in the ineffable, dogma exclusive
to one, lightness after the probing dark
or a by-path, is what?

Barefoot vulnerability
receiving no mercy from edged bones,
the unyielding of earth's memory
calls up a mind's seaborne unloosing
overcoming limits fleshly insistent,
recovering the ineffable

like an albatross soaring
out-riding the inevitable Roaring Forties
of a stormbound past…

Self-examination on a Winding Path

…but the path snakes left
a bump
upslope
underfoot roughening
eyes left see
a long slow shallow pasture-green drop
darkening into wildwood
shot through silver water flashed, winking
in lengthening yellow-pale noon-past light,

and a cloud no bigger than a man's hand.

The path snakes right,
dislodged stones thump
on a down-slope's sharpening,
eyes right; let it be?

A ridge-sprung hop
alerts a greened-darkening world, good
or bad, and only leaf shiver
averts an ominous sinking
into cloud-black up-growth against white
smothering sky brightness
in a dreaming left again turn to lightness.

The path takes on straightness
upsweeping a hill's back,
fear heightens
towards shark-toothed ridges. An attack
of perception tightens
at overspreading darkness,
voices, choices, terrible correctness
holding me to the slope.

The cloud's lope menaces with softness.

Part 3

After the Last Post

Last Post – Anzac Day

They are so head-bowed,
still,
under dawn-expanding skies

a bright/sharp bugle call flies
in counterpoint, midair hovering,
almost dying across wastes
of generations, times,
and memories empowered
by will, ties unbroken
and spectral histories recalled
through overlaying ages.

May history's back turned pages
and the Last Post
uplift their hearts, carrying
across towns and villages
remembrance of deeds
and words once spoken.

'Ghosts, in your time unbroken
fall in, as the sun's first ray
opens the dawn and march today.'

Bypath

After *A Pilgrim's Progress*

Bird songs stilled, cast
into a deafening silence
two steps off the hard shoulder
onto sprung soft underfoot grass
light diminishing but the day no colder
received at last
in a waft of eucalyptus incense
equivocating,
having left a highway foot/ankle hard
none the bolder as the light fades

but found wanting?

Sunset sloping into night
accepts one tired
by edge turning twisting stones
jarred bones
and that calf muscle ache
up-running the thigh
testing the grass, softly,
seeking trees close for nightlong shelter
amid a welter of unwanted questions
voices echoing
crossing the highway…

Nightfall Memories

…and may nightfall memories
be as incense to the soul

beyond the processional goal
arriving…where?

A nightingale sings the night apart,
recollections share
in gathering things lost,
found,

and in darkness
bounding the light
grounding our being, until
transforming
us, for whom the passing bells
toll shades into gathering,
numberless,
still, in a windless night
through hours long vigil.

Waters mirror
a moon-cold light's sublimity
and time breathless, inexorable,
is a passing chime

when night and day each season
of the same coin two-sided, rhyme

a seamless eternity…

Cold Night Bells

…but this night sharply, utterly,
achingly cold
stays the white smoke
of an exhaled breath
under a stellar circumpolar
jewel-encrusted canopy
and a moon full rising
pale washes the dark
diminishing its gold.

I am not sold
on this, or any fresh snow's
underfoot crunching.

Tonal crashes clattering
and wired metallic hammering
of night calling bells
shatter the peace, and a gale
sensationally flails
the awakening self
but does not stoke
its frost fires, now declining

this clatter-toning merging
into a long thin chanting
of midnight watchers voicing
their Kontakion of death
is…from the breath of peace
life-affirming…

Into the Dawn

…into the dawn
white/gold seared, flaring, a virtuoso
toccata of light's
vibrato blending, flinging
a blazing
kaleidoscopic splendour
mingling
light trampling sun-caressing greens
dark-to-light blues
faceted aquamarines tinged violet
and deep earth-softened browns
in spirit born
from the unseen

ineffable creation's shimmer-glow,
a sheen mutated
into flights of iridescence
ringing bird callings, singing
fanned-out glories, grandeurs
of earth, air, fire, enhancing
all in water's self-perpetuating
transcendence

fixed,
transfixed,
on the cross of matter…

Cantilena Pacifica

In memoriam, Richard Meale

…before looking out
over dreaming endlessness
at a slow motion's
beautifully deceptive dappled blue
symphonic ocean's
sea/sky dancing limitlessness,
asking;

'What are your tidal voices singing,
deep truths out-spelling
amid beauty
and devastation
among a thousand islands?'

Flying fish leap – a silver shout
against the sun,
seabirds call/wheel and turn-about
so let them
across a blue/white infinity mark
our memories with understanding
earth/air/sea scenting, sending
vanilla, salt, and coconut tangs
to stir a dormant restlessness;

'But out of what infinite loneliness
call you,
Cantilena Pacifica?'

Beyond the Margin

He walks the streets unbonded
except to himself
wandering
along winter promenades
when spray flicks the railings
and seabirds
skim rough-ridged waves.

Blown sand
and dancing paper packages
fraternise
tossed down dirt tracks
as he tramps with stoic footfalls
towards shelter
and evening fires.

Is this
charitable interdependence
freedom of earth/air
fire/water
the matrilineal quartet?

Beyond the margin
He – the traveller's persona
is socially bereft but harmonised
subliminally
with elemental powers
on a long star road…

The Loneliness of the Long Distance Runner

…until sunlight exposes
from horizon to centre a bleakness
of sand-dusted stones, discloses
a battlefield litter of weathered bones
the shattered technologies of war
over what;
with but one left?

Stranger, say,
'I have run my course
completing my divorce
from material moments undone
across time with history passing
reluctantly, no cover for one
bereft by circumstance
the warp and weft of experience
the lonely destiny
of a long-distance runner
not an emotional daylong flitter
brought on by danger.'

Intrepid ranger: 'Let it be.
Mother Mary waits in the Pass
to the Delectable Mountains
where Arcadian shepherds
drink from the fountains
of Eternity, the soul signs
its Armistice, and journey's end
is less than a horizon away.'

Part 4

There is a River

Autumn Processional

Autumn, processional
seasonal in many guises
is a shape-changer
make-up artist
of extraordinarily transient dexterity,
Andante Con Moto
into sunset singing transitional
blood-scarlet, yellow surprises
turned russet, stranger
than fictional dreaming
diminishing, fading
when light has a clarity of definition
and a coolly sharpening edge

marked *stretto*
when winds pressing the sedge
and water spreading
under sunsets flamed vermilion
black cloud framed
splash-paint,
firing above gold overspreading
pale flashing a rippling *Allegro*
rough-stippling fluidity
into impermanence
and emotion is recollected
not always in tranquillity
falling onto lost opportunities
on leaves way-swept
all over creek and river runs in spate.

Storms early and late
scour land and water
hurrying detritus into time's streaming
accented
world without end
Presto!
Speed frittering away
on colour skittering themes
before a processional *ritardando*
turns recessional
into winter sleep mode's
harvested aftermath,
trees skeletally exposed

earth bared
after high wire balancing
flocking migrant singers
fly into winter's onset
and *Adagio*
is the sky's lead heavy threat.

The Traveller Meets Gregory the Great

A crossing over message whisper-near
enchantment light/word pulsed
entrancement
and a spiritual enchainment
hearing, speaking, singing clear
and alabaster cool
across a sea of visionary silence

be love, like incense
penetrating 'The Cloud of Unknowing',
a *pas de deux* of heart and soul
responding while forgetting
the hardness of a road still stretching
endlessly.

One is; known by voice tirelessly
the Angels Chanter
percolating sinuous, melodic
star streams through the filters of time
materiality
sense and sensibility
engendering in a worn yet warming heart
a comprehension of the infinite.

Recessional Winter

Winter's slow-paced, bleak
Adagio Sostenuto for strings
is long held
starkly overlapping chords
with only
descending harp notes dropping
like frosted ice particles
punctuating *Samadhi*
interlocking a stillness out of time
seeking no ending
or canticles of eulogy

where memories are swords
winter is length, shortness,
life, death and time
slow leaking across hemispheres
solstice capturing
at the Hitching Post
of a retreating sun
turning it back upon itself
as a new moon too weak
against the dark
to rouse a wind's harsh singing
seeks out fires of festival
stomping the boards accelerando
distracting shadow dancing
haunted minds
accentuating
a need for seasonal courtesies,
the bowing in of longer days.

Winter's sun-fire rays
once bleeding evening red
flare briefly white
in cold dawn's dazzling blaze,
and icy brilliance
mutes the heart clock's beat
Allargando
stiff chilled, responding
to Tarot's death card blending
the Reaper's symbols
his living and dying forms
by a sunset river circling
eternally beyond the winter's ice,
calling…

'Let the sleeping seed
dying into rising life
with the iron hard need
of winter met be the strife
of spring's wild onset, freed
from time and rife
with possibilities.'

John Tavener Confronts the Traveller

End is beginning
on a road anywhere
so shelter me somewhere
under 'The Protecting Veil'
hearing a threnody for Athena
and the song of 'The Lamb',
but against the goad everywhere
strike not. I am a tale told,
a dreamer, smaller than a gram.

Agios O Theos
Agios ischyros

I am daring the loss
of humanity's tomorrow but held
between the pillars of The Temple
as the Veil is rending
defying danger
seeing beyond fear the simple
and clear by sorrow unclouded,
unending, un-shrouded
Agios athanatos eleison imas.

Illumine my knowing
since end is beginning.

Spring Rounds

Spring's seasonal resonances
green growing into light
bursting
and water jewel/bright swift
flashing
over winter's monochrome
out-sparking
are breath and blood
Venus ungirdled
Shamanic drumming
and the Rite of Spring

'pulse blossoming
into thunderous flourishes
when root stock multiplying
into dawn light cherishes
the sounding Word, ringing
the changes…'

a *rondo pianistic finale*
beginning the unpredictable
bud into pink/white blooming
briefly flirting colour singing
Allegro Vivace
fulfilling the urge
and sun- powered surge
over water, sound and silence
drum caught
lassoed,
poco rallentando…

'ringing the changes
when a seed self nourishes
the living exchanges
burgeoning from a hidden
thirst for maturation
first into Wisdom.'

Spring will downwind
copper remain in the soil
Venus testify
in star-shaped wanderings
Summer reap her seasonal spoils
Vulcan hold the world
In his toils, and light's

expanding scope around
a Temple's daisy-chain like
dancing unity
anchor hope, when the Temple
of the few becomes
the Temple of the many.

Die Winterreise & *Die Lindenbaum*

The wind's whip, a dithering
Die Winterreise dip in time
no delivering is
from the shivering moment
of the Organ Grinder's discontent
when *Die Lindenbaum* is bare
branch-boned
self unshaded
as you dare to cast
the long chill-bladed
shadow of eternity
first and last
across a five strung-out fraternity,
and once begun
daylong nightlong
standing strong
on a word of challenge,
sharing *Die Winterreise*
prophesy
like a waterfall struck
by a cry from the rock of time
until the last chime
of the last hour…unbarring
a heart's aloneness.

Saraband of Summer

Love beneath the summer stars
between above
and below
coordinating with
the River in the Sky,
celebrations
heat exhaling from embodied earth
into a cooling night
when chanting slows the steps
Andante Molto
of a ritual Saraband

liturgies of heart and hand
of heated blood
drawn down
into a solstice passionless
by step and swing
a poise distilled
before the annealing drought
of long-lit days

when green in many shaded rays
primal deceiver
down-weighs ascension's
evidence
of unseen presences
hopes breathed
out of a land to beige attenuated
and from the stars.

Light and shadow bars
way-goers
by black-towered summer storms
wet and dry
dark, light, fitfully contrasting
clarity and haze,
the Grim Reaper's contradiction
death with life
and seed of everlastingness.

Within the consciousness
of passing days
beyond our solstice time
'*tempo rubato*'
shadows the singing

echoing a summer's ending,
maturation
in the lees of all our knowing
a glass turned down
recessional
and harvest's ceremonial closing.

There is a River

I am a source
summit glaciating into silence
ending, beginning,
potentially descending
into ice melt
in a silence not unfelt
where truth is not emaciating
though coldly intense.

Of force directed I sense
beyond winter's grip
the sun beckoning
in world's ice free, reckoning
on time's unravelling
like a line unwinding
on a centre pin
so walk with me, brother,
in a time like this
no moment other
than the present is
leading from source to sea
feeding the travel worn
the manna of eternity.

Brother, between dying
and being born there is a river…

www.ingramcontent.com/pod-product-compliance
Lightning Source LLC
Chambersburg PA
CBHW070051120526
44589CB00034B/1876